The Soul Collection

of

Moonsoulchild

2 | The Soul Collection

The Journey Through My Heart

To love yourself,

It takes a lot of heart break, losing people you thought you'd never have to live without. It causes you to lose yourself, realizing there's no one you need more than yourself. Don't rush the process. Don't set comfort in places you need to work to be happy in.

Your heart isn't a weapon,

Being heartless is not something to be proud of, it's not something to show off. Being heartless means hiding from the most amazing thing you could ever experience, love. Don't hide from love, don't go out looking for it either. Let love find you. Let yourself feel everything you feel. Your greatest power is to feel every single emotion, accept it or live your whole life blind being heartless, not knowing the true meaning of the best parts of life.

I'm not interested in being liked, understood, or accepted. My worth can't be determined by any of those. I live in a world full of people, who are always trying to make me into someone I don't recognize.

I'm not interested in making anymore lost connections.

I can't believe I ever thought loving myself was selfish.

Message to anyone learning to love themselves,

Self-love doesn't come easy, learning to love yourself is just as challenging as loving others, but more intensely. Loving yourself is so important. Every company you keep until you do, won't be fully conditioned. When you have people around you who help you grow, the ones who help you find you, those are the ones you keep around. You need to surround yourself with the ones who want to see you win just as much as you do. The more you involve yourself with people who half love you, fake love you, and the ones who give you conditional love, the farther away you feel from self-love. You must get rid of the people who don't want to see you win, get rid of the ones who love you in the dark while support people they hate in public. This is not the generation of people with pure hearts. People would rather waste time giving you fake love, while letting you give them your heart. Don't let these people in your life for any reason, they'll make your journey a longer road.
It's so important to keep your aura protected from people who drain your energy and heart from loving people with good hearts. Don't let the demons of your journey bring you fear in accepting the truth in who you are, where you want to be—and where you're at now. Trust the energy you give, and you will receive that

exact energy in return. Love the ones who love you back, unconditionally. Keep the real ones close, while you let the ones who drown your soul of sadness, hatred, in the dark. Let them go. Don't let people who can't love themselves tell you that you can't make it. These people don't define you. Be who you want to be, fiercely. Don't let anyone tell you who you should be, the way you wear your heart on your sleeve is beautiful, I promise that falling in love with yourself is just as beautiful, while having people who love you close, is like having the whole moon in your hands, amazing.

Don't be afraid to be free, to be freely who you are. If you haven't found who that may be, don't be discouraged to stop your journey to self-love because you're not clear on where you're at, or where you're going. Live your life intensely to the point you can't have time to think about analyzing every situation and decision. Be fearless and take on all your fears, weakness, and everything that won't let you fully love yourself. This includes, letting go of people who don't serve you the ways your soul needs. The journey isn't easy, you don't have to, have it all figured out. That's the beauty in life, not knowing what could happen and still hoping you can figure it out. It takes some people forever to find self-love, and some may never understand, my heart goes out to you all, I hope this message can somehow help you understand that your impossible, is possible. Everything you want is well deserved if you go and get it, if you love it deeply and you love you fiercely. Some days you'll hate yourself, some days you'll be obsessed with yourself, and some days you'll be confused. Understand that this is how it all works, you were meant to feel everything you go through, and the greatest one of all will be when you fall in love with yourself.

Don't settle for what you think you deserve, don't just settle for "love". Love isn't waking up one day knowing the one you love, doesn't love you anymore. That's far from love. That isn't love. When you truly love someone, that intimately, you will feel it forever. In this story, forever does exist. Love will always be there and if they say it wasn't, it never was. You can't wake up and just not love someone anymore. But it's possible to outgrow people, change happens in people. But love will always remain. You will meet people throughout your life that you will believe you love, but you won't really love. If you've ever woke up and thought it could be possible to not love them, it's not love you feel. People with good hearts always get confused that's why it's important to be careful who you open your heart to. It's important to protect your heart from who only want you when they want you and gets rid of you when they don't need you.

It's easy for them,

but a person like you with a good heart,

it will scar your heart forever.

I found myself letting go of the people I loved most
when I realized we weren't on the same path. I realized
I couldn't grow with someone who only stunted my
growth. I wouldn't say it was toxic, exactly.
I would describe it as no longer pretending their love
for me was honest.

Someone right now,

Doesn't love themselves like you do, please be kind to them, please let them know they're not alone. Don't ever judge someone based off what they show you, there's so much more to them then what you see on the outside. Their heart is bleeding with the want of love, the kind of love you can only receive from yourself. Keep these ones in mind, keep them close to your heart. It's a crazy mess trying to love yourself in a world of constant reminder of how you can fail at any time.

Love yourself more than those constant reminders.

It's crazy, you know, when people speak on your name so shamelessly. But forget to speak on the pain they've brought upon you, and the reciprocated toxicity of their character. As if they've forgot, they're the reason they view you with so much hurt.

There's nothing wrong with your heart,
sometimes it doesn't understand the first time.

Know what kind of love you receive,
by loving yourself first. Every company you keep after
will make sense.

You'll stop accepting less than you deserve.
You won't allow half love, from half ass people.
You won't tolerate disrespect from people who don't
know you.

Lastly,

Loving yourself will make you untouchable,
It starts with you.

A message to a lost soul:

Don't worry why you haven't gotten to where you want to be already, be blessed to have already gotten to where you are. You can't expect to get everything you've dreamed, without working for it. Do whatever you have to, to accomplish that dream. Some days will be more stressful than others, some weeks will take forever to end, and some may pass quickly you won't remember every detail.

Life is crazy, life is also exciting.

You are life. You are free.

You deserve everything you set your mind to, and let your heart make your biggest dreams come true. Don't ever get comfortable, but always have comfort that you will always make it, you will always find a way. As lost as you may seem now, you'll realize through this whole process, you always knew who you were, you were just too comfortable, you never pushed yourself to your full self. You are a moon in the night sky, beautiful and unreadable, there's nothing wrong with being a mystery to the world, long as you never lose yourself.

You needed me, more than I ever needed you.

I gave all of me, for your need.

Yet I'm the one who's "damaged" the one who's always made out to be the "lost" one.

Under no obligation,

was I meant to fix you, but that doesn't mean I didn't try, instead, I found myself almost broken trying to mend together what wasn't my heartache to recover.

It's always a choice,

You either grow together, or you *outgrow* them.

You're not hard to love,

You just don't love with limitations.
You love with all your soul, or not at all
That's how it should be.
Don't take half love
from people you give your whole heart to.

I've never had the desire to fit in,
I was perfectly made to be different,
I don't have to stand out to prove it,
I've never accepted the opinions
of making me think I was a copy.

When they were upset,
I loved myself more than their judgement.

You grow up learning,
How to treat others,
How to love others unconditionally.
All these years, you grew up learning,
while missing the most important lesson to life
how to love yourself.

Why does it take years to be taught that?

You must own who you are and love you,
To the point everyone's opinions,
Is just noise to your ears.

Everyone I come across,
will have a version of me they'll run with.
Who I am,
will always be unfamiliar, misunderstood, and fixed.
I've come to terms
with letting them run with what makes them satisfied,
Because when it comes down to it,
their version of me is just their illusion.

Love isn't blind, at least to me it's not.
I can truly tell you,
when I've felt love, real love,
there was nothing blind about it
I felt it immediately after facing it.
People let love blind them
using love as an excuse to let no good people,
keep destroying them.

I'm not impressed by the heartless,
I have too much heart, to be cold,
too much love to give, to the ones worth my love.
If my heart disconnects from you,
doesn't intend I'll be cold towards you,
I just learned to distance my heart
away from love that's no longer desired.

Acknowledge the hate that's within you,
before you even try to love me.
This will result in me trying to save you,
and that, will only destroy me, there's no love there.

I Was Never Broken

"A message to an old flame"

I loved you, very much. I'm not sorry about that. Back when it was over, I'd say I was. But now, I thank you. I thank you very much, for showing me what love wasn't. For showing me what it's like to deal with someone who never made my heart skip a beat, but only made it stop beating for you. I look back then, and I see the girl I was, vulnerable, kind-hearted, terrified of heart break, and in complete lust with you. It wasn't until now, I realized I never really loved you. Because looking back, there was never anything to love about you, but the idea. I was in love with, loving you. I was in love with the thought of giving my all to you, hoping that would make you love me back. I was attached to the thought of loving you, I forgot to love you. I see the signs now, the signs I should of ran when I had the chance—the times I always gave in when I should've left. I put my heart out there to get destroyed every single time, and you always chose to destroy. I was so blinded by making sure I had love, I wasn't thinking about whether the love was fully conditioned. My heart was confused. My heart never understood why I kept letting someone like you, in. But I know now, I know why I had to open my heart to you. I know why I needed to give you a piece of me I'll never receive back. Because you know why? It's a piece I won't ever need back. I don't need the pain of getting hurt over and over after putting my heart on the line for you. I don't need that piece of me back. You may savor that piece with you, everywhere you go. Remember me, for everything I was, to you. The love I gave you, the comfort I showed, the trust I had broken every time. I want you to remember me for everything I was, because you will never know who I am today. I suffered for so long trying to end my road with you, it was a blessing finally being able to let you go. You would always come back, months, years, I would be a fool. But I will always remember the day I gave you my final goodbye, to this day, I always wonder how you felt at that moment. But as I'm writing this, I realized I don't care, I don't care how I made you feel because you never cared to wonder how I felt when you chose you every time, over me. And maybe that's it, you chose you, When I should of chose me, every time. Maybe that makes me angry. Maybe it's anger I hold inside of me, Towards you,

Because I couldn't love me enough,

To see right through you.

Some people you meet
are just a part of your road to self-discovery,
Don't let everyone
have a hold over your heart.

I let go of people,
I wanted to keep around forever.
To me, that's become my biggest strength,
If you know me,
You know my hearts big
and my love's unconditional.
If I let you go it was for reasons,
That don't need explanation,
Other than it wasn't me, it was you.

Toxic people are so dangerous.
You'll love them
with all your heart,
without knowing,
your heart is breaking because of them.

If you push me away,
I promise you,
You won't find me where you left me.
My hearts big,
but not big enough to deal with people
who decide to love me
when it's convenient for them.

It's not a loss anymore, to me,
when someone decides to walk out my life.
It's a loss to them,
Having to remember me
for everything I am,
knowing they chose to let me go.

"A message to the old me"

I don't know where to start, honestly. I guess I'll start with saying I'm sorry. I'm sorry for letting you go without the love you deserved. I'm sorry you had to put up with such bullshit from so many people. I'm sorry your heart was too big for some people, but that's the thing about you, you never changed, you always remained true. So, I'm not sorry about that. But I'm sorry you had to get let down, times and times again to show your worth along the way. I know you didn't understand but that was your biggest strength, you always gave all of you without trying to hold back. I'm not sorry you let everyone see your heart so openly, but I'm sorry they ripped it out and slammed it back it repeatedly. I'm sorry you never realized the damage that could've been done. I'm sorry you didn't see them for who they were the whole time. Because that's what it's about, them. They made you forget about you while trying to love them with everything you had while not giving yourself the love you deserved all along, the love you gave so openly. I'm sorry you never understood how important it was to put yourself first. I'm sorry I never helped guide you to the parts of you that needed help. I let you drown in yourself without thinking what the outcome could be. But I know now, I wasn't strong enough to love me back then, like I do now. Every experience, everyone I loved, everything that's shaped me into who I am, had its purpose—and I'm not sorry about that. So, as I remember you, as the shy, over loved soul you were, I'm not sorry, because who you are today, is someone more amazing.

Stop allowing toxic people,
fill you with poison and calling it "love"

"We can all say things, don't mean we all understand."

We can walk the same streets, follow the same signs and still not make it to each other at the same time. We could pour our heart out and tell each other what's going through our mind and still not make it through to each other. We can talk for hours, tell each other how much we love each other, And still not understand why we bother. It's not even you, lately I haven't been feeling like me, I haven't been feeling the vibe of being happy. The whole "smile" isn't real, I just don't know the deal, because lately, I don't even know what's real. I've been chasing too many dreams, too many well "what if", I haven't focused on what's right in front of me, what means something to me. Scared to open and experience something new, something that could help me grow. I cry these tears, tears words can't express; of anger, of depression, of hope, mainly of confusion. Confused on why I'm not as happy as I should. Getting brought down, I always thought I was stronger than that. I lost hope in myself and in every situation. Scared to get close to anyone, what are you really supposed to do, when your hearts not yet broken, but needs repair? It wants love so bad, the love of someone I'm never going to find. Someone I've long to find who will never come into my life only cross my mind. My hearts begging for someone to heal it, just everyone I always thought was right, was wrong. I'm hurt, almost broken, Even though it's not their job to fix me, it's not their crime, they don't need to someone else's time, but it's hard to love someone else without the word PAIN crossing every line. The word TRUST erased from my mind. I know I've done wrong, and this could be karma, God please tell me its karma and it will only last a little longer. I believe I deserve best, promise to never settle for second best. If he doesn't want me to be his first, I won't be at all. I just need someone who will love me for me. When I'm a mess and when I look my best, who cherishes being with me and loves my presence. I just want to be loved in a way it won't have to hurt or I won't have to worry, Because I am everything I am, and that will be enough.

Letters to you

May 28, 2018 7:00 p.m.

I'm so happy I met you, you've taught me what it's like to be free. What it's like to open your heart and love openly, without caring about anything else. You've inspired me to always love, more. I was always fascinated with mystery's, and you found your way to my life—someone who's soft, but not easily open, that's why I was drawn to you. The way your heart cries to the world, the way you wear your heart on your sleeve and have no clue you're even doing it. Thank you for being such a wonderful friend. I've found comfort in you, I've found parts of me that fit with you. I trust the universe, because it gave me you. I'm not easily open, my shell is where I've always resided—and I believe that can make or break any love or friendship I choose to condition. But you, you showed up, right on time, right when I needed you. I thank you for being you. For being the beautiful soul, you are. I only hope you give the world your heart, no holding back. I see you being someone great one day, someone everyone will love, even if they don't see it at first. I know sometimes you might drown in self- doubt, sometimes you might feel there's more you need to do. But listen, you're doing everything perfectly on time—it's not your fault because not everyone's awake, it's not your fault people decide to look the other way. Your love is intense, I've felt a part of it, but it's intensely beautiful. I think that's the scariest part. I just want you to know that nothing you're doing is wrong, it's not your job to wake up anyone who's choosing to sleep on you. Those people will wake up one day and see you, for who you always were, and that's the key to it all. You'll always be you. I just want you to promise me that you'll never change, never choose to change you because not everyone is ready to love you. I will always love you, if that means anything. I will always celebrate you, I will always show the world your heart even if it's hard for you. I'll be your number one fan, because at the end of the day, we all need someone who reassures us on who we are, even if we can't do it ourselves. I just want you to know, that your friendship means the world to me, after losing people in my life who've held my comfort close to them, I get you. Someone who's soft, but not easily open, I'm drawn to you. You'll always be a mystery to me. You'll always be, someone I want more from. But for now, know that, being your friend, has been an honor. I'm so happy to call you my friend.

Knowing you, has been admired,
thanks for letting me in.

July 2, 2018 8:50 a.m.

I want to call this piece "the aftermath" because this is everything I feel at this exact moment. I just read your last piece I wrote, and everything is still accurate. I said some meaningful, insightful things that still make sense, which I figured would. I'm on the plane right now heading back home. I want you to know that leaving you this morning was incredibly hard, I didn't know how to take in this whole weekend, I literally broke down a hand full of times in the car and at the airport. It was just 3 days ago, getting on the plane getting ready to see you, happiness was beautiful, life was amazing. I want to go back to that day first. The anticipation of getting on that plane knowing I was coming to see you, I had no fears, I had nothing holding me back. I know I was coming, I know what I wanted, and I made it happen. I got over one of my biggest fears, well a lot this weekend. I told myself I would never get on a plane, ever in my life. I wouldn't even get on a plane to see my mom when she lived in Georgia. I told my ex I would never get on a plane with him for any vacation. I've surrounded myself with my fears for all my life and I drowned in them, time and time. But for some reason, I had to see you. The universe gave me the "you're safe" green light and I ran with it. My second fear, traveling alone. I barely like to leave my house to go anywhere in town because I get "people anxiety" I hate seeing locals, I hate communicating with just about anyone. But for some reason, you made me feel safe enough to make this journey. And lastly, my biggest fear, was meeting you. Before I came out, I thought about it a million times, I thought how I shouldn't just up and leave my town to go see some man I've never met, in a place I've never stepped foot in. But the ultimate fear wasn't just that, it was facing all these emotions I've held inside me, the feelings I've yet to face head on. In reality. I've been living in my dream world of you. And I'm not saying that what we could have couldn't be real, more like I never thought it could. I know I always go back to the past but it's so hard not to think of everything that brought me to this. You were the light that lead me through the darkness, the light I've never thought I'd see. You eased the pain and made walking away from something I didn't even realize was toxic, you helped me get through that milestone in my life very calmly. I've never met anyone like you. Someone who's soul is just the purest form of beauty. Sometimes I never understand why you were so kind, why you dealt with all my bullshit. But you were always there, and always listened, while having all the right things to say. I could have never done any of this without you. I would have never realized I deserved more until you helped me see the parts that needed to be dead and gone. I know you'll probably take no credit, but I give it all to you. I do believe I deserve more, and more as in the best. I do believe I'm capable of loving myself with the same love I give to others. I do believe that I will be successful one day, very successful, along with making all my dreams come true one day at a time. But can I tell you, ever since I met you, my dreams have been aligning perfectly. I know I made them come true, I know publishing my first book has nothing to do with you, that was all me. But every dream after that, has been inspired by you. And I thank you, for guiding me in the direction I was meant to. And I thank you, for being with me through some of the dreams I've always dreamed, watching them come true. I don't believe I "owe" anything to you, as vice versa. I believe the love we share is enough to show why we do the things we do for each other, and that alone is what makes sense. Everything I do for you, showing your work and your heart to the world, is something I never want to be repaid for, because that's something I kindly do, from the bottom of my heart, because I believe in you. I believe in the you that you can be and are. When you drown in self-doubt, I'll always be here to pick you up from the waves. Not because I must, because I love you too much to watch you drown, knowing you're one of the greatest souls to ever exist. Sometimes we see others in ways we don't see ourselves, and that's the beauty in loving someone, you see them for everything they are, and love them exactly for that reason, flaws and all. So yes, I know you're not perfect, I know you might not be where you want to be in your life at this moment, or not as successful as you wish to be, at this moment. But you are not measured by how much money you make, or what kind of job you have, you're measured by your character and how you show your heart. Your drive for the dreams you make your reality, the heart you show so deeply and intimately to the world. We've all been in a situation where we've been a burden or failed. I've gotten disappointed times and times again. But what I always had, was my heart, and my character never changed through these situations. I know the things I do isn't measured by the amount of money I make, or the things I can provide for another, I'm not the richest person, but I will spend my last to make sure someone I love has what they need. I've spent money so carelessly, well because, there's always more money. Have you ever just sat down and thought about money? And how stupid it is? The amount of money we waste on the stupidest things? Yeah, it's not worth it. At one time in my life I thought money was important, which of course it is, we can't live without it, but honestly, money isn't happiness. Money is the devil that makes us feel as we're not good enough, like we need to impress people with nice things, but that's not how life works, and that's where people always go wrong, that's why they will never understand true happiness. So, I get it, stability is important to you, to be able to provide for another, and give someone you love exactly what they need. But being stable it's not always about providing, it's about partnering. That's just what I've learned. I don't need you to give me the world, because you are that already. There's no amount of money, or material items that could ever amount to you. That's where I draw the line with funds. It's 9:26, and I'm still on the plane, enjoying the view, wishing I was back in your city. Let me get back to the weekend. When you texted, me you were on your way, I had to try and process everything at once, "how am I going to deal" was my first thought. Seeing your face in real life was so scary to think, because I knew I would become a mess. I know things didn't happened as I planned, but every time I think of seeing you on the sidewalk passing you my heart just stopped for a quick second, everything I prayed for had become reality, and I wasn't sure exactly how to face it. That moment was so beautiful. I sit here and repeat it over and over in my head and it makes me happy, yet sad at the same time. I literally cry tears of happiness and sadness at the same exact time and the shit is so confusing. I thought getting on that plane was enough for me to be prepared, until I seen your face and I was lost. I couldn't even look at you because it all felt like a dream. This whole weekend was a dream, one I never wanted to wake up from. A beautiful dream that became a reality, for one weekend, amazing. It was exactly what I wanted, and a bit more. To see you, in the real, was exactly how I pictured you. No fantasyland can beat reality you. You are so much more real than any daydream I've created of you, you are so much more than any fantasy I've created. I wasn't disappointed, not once. Everything was exactly how I pictured it would be, and it was all equally amazing. It was all so natural. It felt like we've known each other for years, when it's only been two months. I felt so safe in your presence, and so open to be me, without fear. I've never once felt that in my life. I've always held a little back just to make others comfortable, but you, you make being me so easy, because you're you and you accept me perfectly. You see me for the person I am, and I can't thank you enough for letting me be in your presence this weekend and making me feel whole once again. Not saying I don't feel whole alone, because I'm secure, I'm very capable of being alone. But just because I can be alone doesn't mean I don't have a piece missing that needs filling. You are that piece. You are the perfect fit. That's all I keep thinking. All I keep thinking is "why isn't this possible" if you're the perfect piece? That's where I'll always get lost. Maybe that's where I'll end up disappointed. But at this point, disappointment is the least of my worries. I'm just trying to make sense of the mess I made, the mess I've created within my own heart and my own head. I know regardless of what happens between us we'll always be friends, even though it will be the hardest thing to do, it's better than having to live life without my best friend. The one person who gets me like no one else does, and when I say that, I mean it completely. I've never connected with anyone on this level, a day in my life. It's a beautiful high, a high no drugs could amount to. You're my high. This weekend was the greatest weekend of my life, now it's a part of a memory. A beautiful memory. I only hope to make more memories with you. I only hope to see you again and enjoy more of your presence. This weekend proved we didn't need to do anything, we completely enjoyed each other's presence and that alone is a lot to do. I completely enjoyed doing nothing but talk with you, pure happiness. From getting to admire your face, to seeing that beautiful smile, to see you truly happy, was everything I prayed for. I only prayed this weekend was nothing less than perfect, and the universe aligned our paths perfectly and I can't thank you enough for giving me all of you this weekend. I can't thank you enough for letting me give you all of me, and you knew exactly what to do with me. I can't thank you enough for going to sea world with me and seeing the whales for the first time and enjoying every minute with me. It's so crazy how you never made anything about you, how you gave that day to me completely, and I've never had that ever, because I'm too much the same and that's exactly my ways of doing. But we balance each other out, and that's beautiful. I'm not sure if I must even talk about the love making, it pretty much spoke for itself, but I adore how it was more than just sex, how you made it more than anything I've ever had, intimately. I never knew talking during sex was a thing until you, and how beautiful it can be. I will miss those moments. Looking into your eyes while you gave me all of you, I found myself deep in your soul, and at times I wanted to break down because I knew that I'd have to disconnect, but I lived how I wanted to in that moment and it was everything. I've been working on the living in the moment instead of picturing the future, and it's been beautiful. I only pray that there will be more one day, because there isn't no one else I want, and I know I haven't lived, I haven't met enough people to see. But I don't want to, I don't overlook any feeling I get when it's this raw. I have met my soulmate and I promised myself I would never overlook that when I came face to face with it. I know this is a lot of pressure on your part, but please don't feel pressure. I don't want you to feel anything but what you feel. Whether or not we become one, one day, I still have you, and the greatest memories of my life, and I thank you for letting me get the chance to love you, and the chance to be able to experience a piece of life with you. Watching the office with you, to being complete freaks the next minute, to talking deeply about our feelings, about life, and about everything. You are my bestfriend, I hope you know that. I admire every part of you. To you singing the whole car ride back to your house, to you being with me to make a dream of mine come true when you could have found something better to do, I admire your soul. I admire you dancing in front of the tv while eating pizza. I could have never imagined someone who was so perfect. I love ALL of you. All "three" of you, equally. I admire how you make me laugh. I admire how you make me smile. I admire how happy I just am, in your presence. I admire the safeness you bring when I'm around you. All my fears, all my worries, everything didn't matter this weekend, my focus was you, and only you. I know I'll find more to say, but for now, I'm going to go. But please, know that this was amazing. I wish I could have stayed forever. And yes, the future is where it's at, and right now all we have is the moment, but I will pray to God every night that someday, this moment will turn into the future. Because there's no one else out there, that will ever make me feel the way you do. And I say this with completely honesty, you are everything and more, please know that. Please know that you are my favorite person. I love you my love.

July 7, 2018 4:25 a.m.

I'm thankful for every girl
who chose to overlook you.
I'm thankful,
they weren't meant to fit with you
we were meant to align perfectly,
you were meant for me,
every part of you
was made to fit with me.
You're mine,
nothing can compare,
to the love we've created.

"God, please protect him from the pain of anything that's out to get him. Please keep him healthy, happy, and forever loved. Please show him that who is his, is someone who deserved to be loved, with the love I've got to give. Please make sure he knows how special he truly is. Because I plan on making this last a lifetime, and I just pray he's ready for it. Because there's no one else I'd rather spend every day with, than him. I give you my word, God, I promise to never do wrong by him. By giving him my heart, I'm giving him all of me, knowing I can be broken at any time. I'm giving him the same energy I want reciprocated. I promise to never hurt him, but only protect him from the world when it's a dark place. I promise to save him from himself when he's in need of it. His love makes me feel like I can do anything, and I will give him everything. So please, God, can you protect us. I need you to make sure we're good. Because I don't ever want to lose this kind of love. I don't ever want to wake up one day and lose this. I pray that this will always make sense, that we won't ever have to look the other way, because we'll find new ways to fall deep in love over and over, for eternity. Amen"

July 13, 2018 1:03 p.m.

I crave a love that's deeper than the ocean,
a love that's beyond the moon.

I crave the love that's inspired by you.

July 15, 2018 2:26

The love you give to me, along with the love you inspire within me, is the kind of love I've been praying for my whole life. *Your love sets all past love to shame.*

The Journey Through My Heart
Part II

You tried and tried to show your love,
but they took until you had no more to give.
They never saw you for the beauty you could be.
Instead, they saw you as the mess you were,
within the mess they've made.
You were never enough for them
even though you've proven
you're everything they need.

Falling in love with yourself
is terribly hard when you know your flaws downfalls and what you wish to change. Compared to falling in love with someone, they love the parts you view as flawed. That's the beauty in love, finding someone who helps you see the beauty in you.

Love,
real love,
will surprise you at the time you least expect it.
You won't be looking for it,
it will show up ready to reciprocate the same energy.
Love that love with everything
that's the love that deserves you.

Never let your heart turn cold,
you owe it to yourself to keep loving.
Being cold will only bring you pain
find the warmth in your heart.
Your love deserves to be felt,
you have too much heart to be cold
just because you live in a world
that's afraid to show their heart.

A love that's real,
won't ever change or outgrow you.
A love that's real,
will grow with you
it won't ever make you believe you don't deserve it

Self-love is the hardest chapter in your life to uncover.
There is so many dimensions
to loving every part of you.
Accepting your flaws and how they tie into your beauty.
Letting go of old habits that created toxic behavior.
Bringing in the new
the growth, and lastly, the love.

Falling in love with someone based on who they are
and how they make you feel is a love that's true.
Falling in love with someone because you're lonely
and the idea, will only bring you pain.
Don't force falling into love
it's a beautiful miracle when it finds you.

I pray whatever is holding you
from being genuinely happy,
passes quickly and you learn how important it is
to love yourself
with every piece of you that feels broken.

"The grass isn't always greener on the other side"
doesn't mean you have to stay
on the side the grass doesn't grow.

Falling in love with someone, you had no intentions on falling for, is the most beautiful kind of love.
No forcing chemistry or trying to save them.
Just a pure, raw connection, that created on its own.

I pray you find someone
who matches your energy and soul
the exact amount needed
to fulfill that missing piece.
Before you find them,
I pray you find you.

Sadness did not consume my life in a whole. Sadness would come and go, more so in waves, then it chose to stay more often than I anticipated. Now, happiness has come into my life to stay, I have parted ways with my dark days. Those dark days are far behind me, as all I'm left with are the memories of broken promises, broken dreams, and disappointments of false hopes. I let sadness consume me of my time. I let sadness consume me of my energy. I let sadness become my reality. Sadness contained most of my memory, As I only told stories about lovers who spoke more than they have ever set action to. I wrote stories how my love was too intense for anyone who touched my heart. I was too much of a woman back then, I was too much of a wholesome lover, to ever be loved back then. No one in my past was ready for my love. The kind of love I gave, was the kind of love the moon gave the night sky, the way it lit through the darkness. I guess what I'm saying is, my love shined too bright to heal anyone I have loved, because my job was not to heal them, my job was to love them, love them enough in order to find the piece of me within them. The piece of me that added to the story of finding me. It might sound selfish, to pick up missing pieces within lovers, old friends, and old flames, but I have come to understand, there is a piece of us in everyone we have a connection with, and those pieces add to our story. Every disappointment, I have paid my dues. I have written my wrongs within everyone I disappointed. Everyone who has done me wrong, I forgave. Everyone I did wrong, I let them go. No one I ever hurt was intentional, and truly, my heart would never hurt the one I love, that is just the way the story played out. Maybe I never loved you the way my heart needed in the first place, but I sure loved you in ways that made sense until our story ended. I accepted, people were written into our lives, and to never question the intention, to be open to love, be open to understand the purpose of the love that surfaced in the first place. I,never forgot the love I held for ones I let free, to this day I still hold love within my heart for ones who planted their seed within my heart but never grew, because, for some reason, it was not meant to. At the time I never knew the love would not grow, I did not know our story would end slow. That is the scariest part, as I reflect on my life, I find myself wondering where I went wrong with one's I thought I would hold close to my heart. I realized it was never my fault, whether I was done wrong, or it was my wrong, the universe knew that love was not the kind of love my heart could handle, because it was only out to destroy me. I picked up the pieces many times, within lovers who let me give more than they wished to reciprocate. I had lovers who never gave but loved to watch me drain my love to consume them. I had lovers who loved me back, but never loved me enough. As I say, loved me back, but never enough, there was always more for me. I had too much heart, to give someone half. I had too much heart, to let someone think it was right to only reciprocate half their love, while watching me drain myself to become someone of their need. I picked up the pieces many times. I watched myself fall apart as I fixed them. I tried saving them, while completely losing myself. My heart survived. I cried a thousand times. I became a fool to everyone I let love me but somehow I made myself out to be the bigger one. That's the thing, about people with good hearts, we always give more, without realizing the importance of getting the same energy reciprocated. Having a good heart is dangerous, because you find yourself in the circle of unrequited love. That's when I learned, just because you love someone, doesn't mean you are meant to. Just because you love someone doesn't mean they are someone you need to keep in your life. Sometimes you need to love someone enough to let them go. People will take until you have no more to give. There's no fixing them, there's no making anyone understand what your love's like. After all the hurt, all the time you wasted trying to rekindle love that set the flame to fire, as you slowly watch that fire burn out. A real one, will walk into your life, and they will feel it. You will feel it, nothing will be said. Happiness will consume you like sadness never could, it will love you in ways sadness couldn't. Let happiness be your light. Let happiness plant that seed within your heart and let it grow this time. Because now, I loved myself enough to let go of everything that consumed me of me, as I watch the old me fade into the background, I watch the new version of me become the woman I dreamed to be. I will let happiness take control of my life. My dark days are over. Sadness, I know you'll always find a way back in, but I will never let you stay, I will never let you consume me of making me believe people who do not really deserve me, have any right loving me in ways they could never amount to. Sadness, I know it is time, we say our goodbyes, I just want you to know, having someone who loves me back is incredible, more than chasing someone who never loved me ever could be. I'm tired of trying to show my heart to ones who do not deserve the time, while I can give my heart to someone who appreciates my time. I was lost for a long time, but I connected with me again, and happiness and me, we are a thing. It is time, to say goodbye, you consumed me of too much time, thinking I was blind, thinking I was not enough, but listen, you were just another fool, I was made out to be the bigger one when I thought you'd fill me up with your remedy. This time, the jokes on you, I'm too good for you.

Sadness, you're now in the rearview mirror,
I have no vision of you.
Hello happiness, I'm so ready for you.

I wasn't interested in being accepted, especially when it came to a crowd I didn't fit into. I never forced a connection with people who never felt me. I might have misunderstood my purpose, I might have chased for love, but I never made someone feel like I needed them. I never felt the need of someone like the need to find myself and love me. I never thought someone could fill me with the courage to love myself, the way I could pitch my own voice, and love me with every part of myself I took for granted. I wasn't interested in being someone's doormat, but that didn't mean I never let people stay longer than their time granted, I can't lie and say I didn't try to make things work when they were way overdue to be outgrown. I can't say I never let someone walk all over me and made me believe their love was something I lived and breathed, I kept letting ones open me up just to fail me. I never said I'd give up, sometimes I had too much pride, sometimes I had too much heart, I couldn't give up anything that I promised I'd take to the grave. I couldn't tell you why I chose to let people come and go when it was time to be real. I couldn't tell you why I tried to keep people around who weren't a permanent stay. I couldn't tell you why I thought loving myself wasn't important when it came to letting everyone else touch my heart—I never understood how my love for them could be honest if I couldn't even be real with myself. I never had the same love for myself. The importance of my self worth was out the window when it came to my worth within lives I held no purpose in. I couldn't tell you why I fought wars with people who spoke on me like I wasn't worthy, but I couldn't stand up for myself because I didn't know my worth. I never said I was confident, when it came to myself, I never knew how important I was because everyone else was more important. I fought love for years trying to understand why no one loved me the same I prayed to be, the whole time I was praying to be loved, but couldn't understand the only way I could be loved, was to condition my love within myself. I stood for much, yet I could never stand for anything when it came to speaking on the love I knew I didn't deserve, but still let consume me. I was weak for so many people, I let them destroy me with their fire, while watching me burn without trying to revive me. I was once the same kind of toxic I was consuming, I never put myself first, I let myself become destroyed, to the point I was almost broken. I never said I didn't think about falling apart, I just thought about the pieces and the amount of time trying to mend myself together. No one had the strength to break me, I take pride in knowing no one has what it takes to make me feel as I'm worth breaking. I wasn't interested in making connections that lead me no where. I wasn't interested in putting my heart into something that wouldn't give me a story. I wasn't interested in wasting a moment trying to be understood by someone who couldn't understand. I wasn't interested in being told my worth from people who couldn't even love themselves. It wasn't my thing, to be within a crowd that thought I wouldn't be someone, someone other than a fool, because I know they always saw me being someone, but never someone more than them. To everyone who doubted me, I pray you find your closure within these words, now I'm somebody more than you thought of me. I'm now somebody I knew I would be. To everyone who once played my heart, I pray you find someone who loves you the exact

when you need, because I couldn't. I couldn't love someone who made me feel like it was impossible to love myself— because neither could you. To everyone I once loved, I pray you're good. Because I once loved you, but no longer hold that love within me. I'm more than a misunderstood woman who couldn't be felt, who couldn't be loved for who I am, but always loved. To everyone I called a friend, those days were long ago, I'm not saying they aren't remembered, I'm just saying there's more I wish to forget, than I wish to remember. I pray you've found your peace, and the you, you've hoped to be. To everyone who reads this, I'm somebody now, someone I always knew I was but was terribly scared to be, I cared too much about what I was made out to be than what I loved about me.
I love me now,
I'm not interested in loving anyone more,
then I love me.

"When do you know it's time to let someone go"

When I gave all of me
to the point there was no more to give.
When they didn't question when I became distant.
All the chasing trying to prove my love
when they decided not to chase me back.

I am mature enough to forgive people in this lifetime for the times they treated me less because their insecurities shined brighter. I am mature enough to see the difference in hate, and someone who is just lost. I was once foreign to myself, so if you treated me wrong, under the circumstances, I forgive you. I pray you are at a place in your life where you are happy and at peace, or if you are still soul searching, I pray you are closer to identifying. I am mature enough to know sometimes we love people who were only meant to be a moment. I am mature enough to not hold regrets towards the same people who brought me more pain than love. I am always praying for love, happiness, and peace, for everyone who I loved and lost. Our paths no longer meant to align, while our souls found a deeper connection within. Where we were headed never matched, just like our souls, it only made sense until it no longer did. The love still holds weight over my heart as you will always be remembered, but I am mature enough to know the difference in loving and letting go, and how important to know sometimes you feel both. I am mature enough to admit I held some toxic traits too, and how I let myself be consumed by you. I am mature enough to admit I was not perfect, I brought pain too. I am mature enough to admit to everything you want of me, but I cannot say the same for you, and until then, you will never find peace where you desperately try to.

Instagram- moonsoulchild
Twitter- moonssoulchild
Facebook- moonsoulchild

Made in the USA
Columbia, SC
01 June 2021